LIGHT FROM THE YELLOW STAR

Light from the Yellow Star

A Lesson of Love from the Holocaust

ROBERT O. FISCH

FREDERICK R. WEISMAN ART MUSEUM

UNIVERSITY OF MINNESOTA

Director's Preface

It is a great pleasure to present the work of a member of our University community, Robert O. Fisch, during our inaugural year at the Frederick R. Weisman Art Museum at the University of Minnesota. David Brown of the University's Medical School first brought the work to my attention in the fall of 1992, just as the walls of our new facility were rising above the banks of the Mississippi River.

Despite the overwhelming task of opening a new building, the staff felt strongly about presenting this project, and I am grateful to all of them for willingly taking on extra work to make it a reality. Kathleen Fluegel, the museum's director of development, our curator, Patricia McDonnell, and Kay McGuire, museum store manager, worked particularly hard to make not only the exhibition, but also the publication of this book, a reality. Stephen Cogil and Emilie Buchwald were early and enthusiastic supporters of the project, and Don Leeper of Stanton Publication Services has been a patient and professional collaborator.

Erwin A. Kelen, founder of the Yellow Star Foundation, generously took on a major portion of the fundraising for the project, enabling us to go ahead with the publication. Polly Nyberg and Mary Pickard of the St. Paul Companies greeted the project with both interest and enthusiasm. In addition, I would like to thank the following individuals, foundations, and corporations, whose financial support has made this exhibition and publication possible:

Betty and Marvin Borman
Babe Davis
Ronald Eibensteiner and Laurie Steinfeldt
Linda and Mike Fiterman
N. Bud and Beverly Grossman
Leo and Doris Hodroff
Miriam and Erwin A. Kelen
Delores and Sheldon Levin
Rhoda and Tom Lewin
Lieberman-Okinow Foundation
Edith and George Nadler
Lawrence Perlman
Rose and Jay Phillips Family Foundation
Stacy and Donna Roback
Ruth and Harold Roitenberg
The St. Paul Companies
Carol and Frank Trestman
Penny and Mike Winton

Frederick R. Weisman Art Museum
Lyndel King, Director

UNIVERSITY OF MINNESOTA

In memory of my father and others
who were persecuted for their faith

With thanks to Anna and all those
who risked their own lives to help save my mother and others
because of their own beliefs

To my daughter, Rebecca Alexandria, and to all children,
whom I love because of my faith in them

And to my friends,
who had faith in me

These Words Are Their Flowers—"They Were Killed by Hatred; Their Memory Is Kept Alive in Love."

I have been thinking for quite a long time whether any medium is appropriate to describe the scope of the tragedy of the Holocaust. How can sorrow, suffering, and atrocities of this magnitude be expressed? With this book I want to say that it is not the ugliness of hate but the beauty of love which survives in time. History is the result of human emotion, conflict, and interest. The purpose of this book is not to make a memento of this horror but to know it and to learn from it. We need to find out how to prevent the occurrence of such a tragedy again and how to be human beings in all circumstances. We must develop principles of belief which provide a good quality of life, with self-respect as well as respect for others and by others. The Holocaust teaches this lesson: "Love overcomes hate."

I was 18 years old, living in Budapest, Hungary. My mother worked from 3 a.m. until 6 p.m., six days a week. Her favorite saying was, "A man is as good as his word." From her I learned determination, endurance, and responsibility. My father, an exceptionally good man, loved life and always helped others. His favorite saying was, "Live and let live." From him I learned compassion and laughter. He and I had unlimited joy together. I admired my father above all other human beings. Our parents provided my brother and me with every kind of education, and with things they were not fortunate enough to have had in their youth.

I had just finished high school and was getting ready for further studies. Because I was a Jew, I was not accepted at the university. Instead I attended evening classes at an art school. (My older brother was sent to Switzerland to study and to be away from the political turmoil.) From my infancy, I had a devout Catholic nurse named Anna, who lived with us through the years and became like a second mother to me, providing me with unlimited love and kindness. I attended both Friday service in the synagogue and Sunday Mass. I was taught to respect others' beliefs and ways of life, and our door was always open to those who were less fortunate.

Buda and Pest are separated by the River Danube, but bridges connect them. So it was in my home: different religions were linked by love and understanding.

"I heard the news; I trembled and became speechless."

On March 19, 1944, when the Germans occupied Hungary, my life and the lives of many others changed forever. Soon after the occupation, all Jews had to be identified on their clothing with a large yellow Star of David. Their property was taken away, and they were moved to the ghettos. I volunteered with an organization that served as a liaison between the Jews and the German commandant. I was working in the Country Division.

One day, a very excited man came and wanted to be seen by the top delegate. He described the first loading of Jews into boxcars: they were jammed shoulder to shoulder, squeezed together, without food or water, with only the clothes on their backs. The doors were locked from the outside, and the trains were heading toward an unknown destination. Although I knew nothing about the fate of Jews elsewhere in Europe, from that moment on, I knew that my only hope for the future lay in the American forces occupying Sicily, the imminent invasion in France, and the advancing Russians from Stalingrad. When the bombs started dropping on Budapest, I knew that survival would require sacrifice.

"Outside, we were destroyed by weapons; inside, by terror."

January 1945: We were now with many others near the Austrian border. Imagine the oval brick burner building with its small opening filled with crawling skeletons. For two nights, we were forced to stay in the furnace room. The smell of decomposing bodies and incineration containers full of human excrement was indescribable. In the darkness, we had no way to distinguish the dead from the dying. Millions of lice had invaded us. What a hopeless fight—fingers exhausted from endless scratching and nails broken by futile smashing. This point marked the beginning of an epidemic. My suspicions about our destiny were confirmed.

"Death rushed through our windows."

An epidemic of typhus, a disease transmitted by lice, broke out two weeks later. I was the first one to have a high fever; then many prisoners started to collapse, one after another, unable to walk. The Germans reacted by kicking them, but soon realized there was an epidemic and set up a room for the sick. The doctor sent for me and said, "You have to stay in there."

"Not me," I said; "I would rather work, even with the fever." The food was wonderful for the sick ones, since it included chocolate, an unimaginable luxury item. Oh, how tempting it was!

Twenty-nine people were confined to the sick room. One day, two trucks came to pick them up. The driver said, "Come on, there's room for 30 in the hospital where I'm taking these people."

"Fisch," the doctor said, "you're the sickest; come." But I did not go. I did not trust them. The doctor told me I was crazy not to go and said that he never wanted to see me or hear my complaints again. Many who were well volunteered to go to the "hospital," but only one "lucky" one was chosen to be number 30.

All were shot at the edge of the village.

"The songs of the sanctuaries turned into screams."

In the dead of winter, we marched from dawn to sunset at the foot of the Alps. Sometimes we marched for days without food or water. If someone sat down, he was shot. We carried nothing. Blankets were acquired by picking one up off the ground where it lay after someone had dropped from fatigue and no longer needed it. As we climbed toward the mountain pass, the number of bodies increased. We were ordered to stop and form lines of five. At the pass, two were randomly shot from each line. As some fell, the rest kept marching.

"Oh, God, in my sorrow, I turn to Thee."

We reached a small village by late afternoon. We numbered thousands, hungry and exhausted. An Austrian peasant brought a bag of apples to the edge of the fence and started to throw them toward us. The reaction of the prisoners was wild. But the peasant paid a dear price: she was shot on sight.

Yet the SS members sometimes surprised us with their actions. Together they performed their duties without hesitation, whatever the cruel or vile act. However, alone, when not seen by their comrades, some of them behaved quite differently indeed. For instance, once during a march, an SS soldier rudely broke the line, then secretly handed out sandwiches. On another occasion, the soldiers "mistakenly" gave out more food than the ration permitted. Humanity can be seen even in such a place as this! It was as if rare vegetation had appeared miraculously on a rock.

"How the heroes were falling!"

We arrived at Mauthausen, an old concentration camp where the gas chambers were out of service. A big sign hanging above the entrance read, "Work Makes You Free." Dead bodies and skeletons were sprawled all over. Food ration for a day was a cup of black coffee and a quarter slice of dark bread covered with green fungus. The toll was evident in our physical appearance—gaunt faces and skeletal frames. One dying boy turned to me and asked me to tell him about restaurants. "Is it really true that you can eat as much bean soup as you wish?" He never found out.

We slept in huge circus-sized tents. How marvelous to be in a tent after weeks of marching, with nowhere to lay our heads but on the frozen ground under the sky. The entire camp was surrounded by electrical barbed wire and towers with reflector searchlights shining penetrating beams across the grounds all night. In Germany it was forbidden even to light a cigarette at night because of air defense. On our second night there, a bomb was dropped and exploded in my tent. The airplane noise was deafening; all around were injured people, fire, bloodshed, and death. I was in a deep sleep and drooling. I awoke and thought, "Aw, who cares? What a way to go!" I turned over and went back to sleep.

"Behold my misery and save me."

We started out on yet another march because the Russians were nearing the camp. Five days of marching, and we were less and less able to walk because of our diminished strength. Some were given help and put on couches rigged to horses. Our destination: Concentration Camp Gunskirchen—a "gem" in the Austrian forest. The exhausted victims from the couches were thrown directly into open graves, then killed.

The barracks were packed full of people squatting—one on each side of you, one in front of you, knee to knee, one in back of you—crammed together. We were confined to the barracks 12 hours at night. During the night, some of the weaker prisoners toppled over, burying others underneath, so that many suffocated. During the day, we were lined up and counted three times, for two hours. Food was given to us from a barrel the SS stood in. Our breakfast was a cup of coffee; our dinner, a cup of soup and a slice of bread. The toilet facilities consisted of a room for 12 men and 16 women for a prison population of 30,000. You had to use the "facilities" when you could find time to go—when you were not standing in line or confined to your barracks. Diarrhea or constipation afflicted everyone. Those who could not wait to use the toilet were executed on the spot.

One day an unusual alarm sounded, and everyone was ordered out of the barracks. The SS announced that someone had eaten meat. Who did it? Meat? Here? Ahh, they had eaten part of a corpse. Declaring what an "inhumane act" this was, the SS shot the perpetrators in front of us to "teach us respect for the dead ones." Oh, what a lesson in humanity.

"Like dawn in the darkness, Thy light arises."

We were finally informed that Berlin had been occupied on May 1, 1945. Joy and hope filled our hearts, but nothing changed. It was "business as usual" with even more death. Following such feelings of hope, our despair became more profound than ever. The end seemed so close, yet so far away. A few SS tried to escape, and the others lost no time in hanging them.

Our leaders learned that there existed an order: If enemy troops were approaching, the prisoners would be machine-gunned and the camp burned down. We made a deal with the guards: some of us went to meet the approaching Americans and bring them in.

May 4, 1945, the Americans arrived! The young men from overseas risked their lives and saved ours. They were liberators bringing freedom and the beginning of an unexpected new life. What a relief it was to see their kind faces as they threw food, clothes, and candy to us. I had to crawl to pick anything up, since I could not bend down and still keep my balance. The vanguard American troops—who had fought the Germans all the way from Normandy until they met the Russians in the East—even they were puzzled by our situation. They couldn't believe their eyes or our stories. Who could? Who could believe that we suffered our "Calvary" only because we had a different religion?

"Even death could not come between us."

I learned that my father had been taken away. Even in the camp, he gave his food to the needier ones, explaining, "I always have enough." He hoped to meet with me along the way, but our paths never crossed. He was remembered as saying, "If one man can do this to another, there is no reason for me to go back." And he didn't come back. My beloved father, who always gave to others, starved to death. What had become of "Live and let live"? He was so greatly respected in the camp that he was the only one not buried in a common grave.

After the war, an eyewitness told me all this and led us to his grave. We brought him back, and he was the first to be buried in the Jewish Memorial Cemetery for the Martyrs in Budapest.

"And the whole country mourned—
families and individuals."

Out of 280 men, only 120 were still alive. The number had decreased that much in only three months. On my 20th birthday, I had to crawl over a single step because I was too weak to walk up on it. My hatred of the Germans was simple: "I will kill them all!" Then on encountering my first German as a free man, I had to make a choice. He was dirty and hungry, begging for food. I asked myself whether I should do to him what they had done to us, or if I should do what my father would do. . . . I gave him some food.

When I arrived home in Budapest I found my mother alive. Anna and her family had given her refuge. But my father wasn't home, and all of my other relatives had vanished (except for my brother, safe in Switzerland). Out of 600,000 Hungarian Jews, only 80,000 had survived.

"Because of them, our eyes are full."

They say that one man's death is a tragedy, 100 a disaster, 1,000 a statistic. At a memorial concentration camp cemetery there are many gravestones. As people walk through it they see one stone that reads, "Here are 10,000"; another reads, "Here are 20,000"; and so on. At the exit is a stone that reads, "Here is one."

According to the Talmud, the book of Jewish tradition, God created Adam alone in order to teach us the importance of life. "The destruction of a single life is like the destruction of the entire world." The loss of more than one person, even if multiplied by 6 million, cannot be measured in mathematical terms. The death of my father was the death of the world as I had known it before.

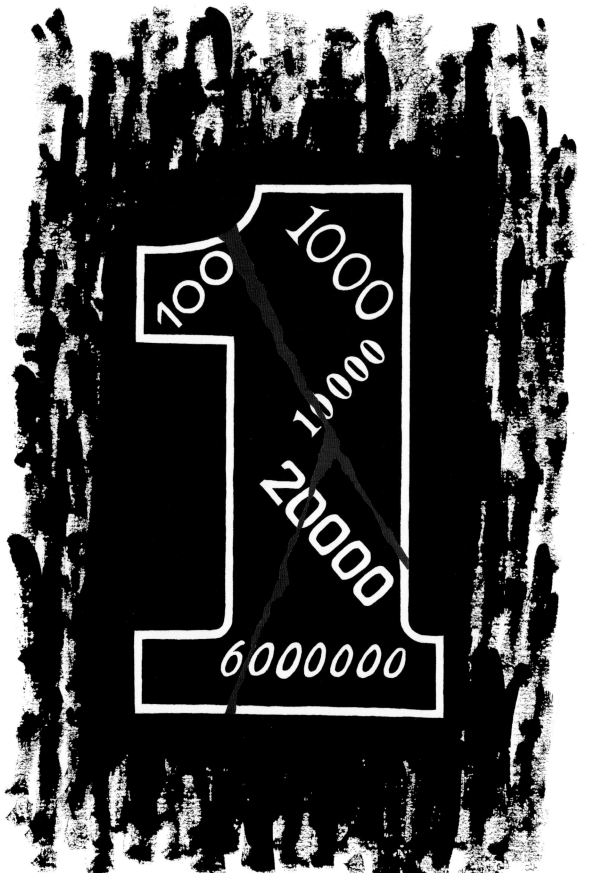

"Those martyrs live."

How can the suffering and death of 6 million people be illustrated and appropriately described or expressed? What can we learn from it? In the case of tyranny, the individual has to stand up and fight. You become part of either the suppressors or the suppressed. There is no third way. No one nation can take all the blame, nor can another be the only victim; all humanity shares in both the guilt and the sacrifice.

The impact on all of us who survived remains in our experience. Whether we recognize it consciously or unconsciously, it is like a shadow accompanying us to our graves. I rarely think about it; however, I did gain insights. To me, bread is a symbol, as it is for Catholics. For them it is a symbol of the body of Jesus; for me it is a symbol of life. It is such a joy to go to the grocery store and buy food. (Remember the boy who wanted to eat a second order of bean soup?) Nights are a different story. As a European-born writer in Israel said, "We might win all the battles against the Arabs during the day but lose against the Germans every night." At night I died a hundred times.

I feel that all of us who were marked by the yellow star were tatooed inside. We have a special obligation, not a privilege, in being alive. As survivors, our moral and human obligations are essential, and our standards have to be based on human principles rather than on practicalities. We must take a stand against suppression and injustice. It hurts me more when injustice is done by Jews than by others. I do not have any hatred. I did not become a judge, even though I was a victim. Now I have a special obligation to show that my life is more than survival. We who survived are not different from others; we just played a special role in a special time.

One night in a dream I asked God, "Are we the chosen people?"

"The world turns on its axis and each segment receives an equal share of sunshine." That was the answer.

"After all of this, should not the world tremble and every person mourn?"

My paintings are usually joyful; through them I want to show how life could be, rather than what it is. I have painted the illustrations in this book because I felt that, as one who was there, I could justifiably attempt to describe the desolation of those who were part of the Holocaust.

In one painting I use barbed wire to illustrate ghettos, concentration camps, isolation. Even outside there is no hope. The shred of the yellow star represents being branded and tattooed. It suggests loneliness, deprivation of dignity, and the residue of the survivors; tattooed persons become merely numbers in a sequence, impersonal objects, no longer individuals. Red typifies the existence of horror, torture, suffering, bleeding. Black symbolizes hopelessness, despair, death. Even after death there is no peace. Each line, form, and color is a different shade of sorrow.

"Even the stones weep."

In the memorial cemetery where my father is, walls with the names of those whose whereabouts are known by location contain quotations. By including some of these quotations (in liberal translation) here, I have tried to give the illusion of walking with me in the cemetery to share how I felt and what I felt among the weeping gravestones—in reality and in my dreams.

Let these words be the flowers for those who did not return.

As beautiful pearls are produced by the suffering of an oyster, so the Holocaust created beautiful heroes—not only among the victims and survivors but also among the others who risked their own lives in order to help those who were persecuted and to save their lives—people like my old nurse, Anna, and her family.

Even among the most sorrowful memories, the humanitarian acts performed by compassionate individuals shine above the dark side of brutality.

I wrote this book because good can be learned even from one of the worst human tragedies. In life—and even in death—the human spirit, love, and fine principles lead the way for the survivors.

When we reach the end of our days and make an inventory of our actions, we should conclude: "I did the right thing—for myself and for others. My time was spent well and my life has been valuable and worthwhile." We have to make a choice either to become a suppressor, taking advantage of the misery of others, or to remain humane even in an inhumane environment.

The light from the yellow star should always remain with us.

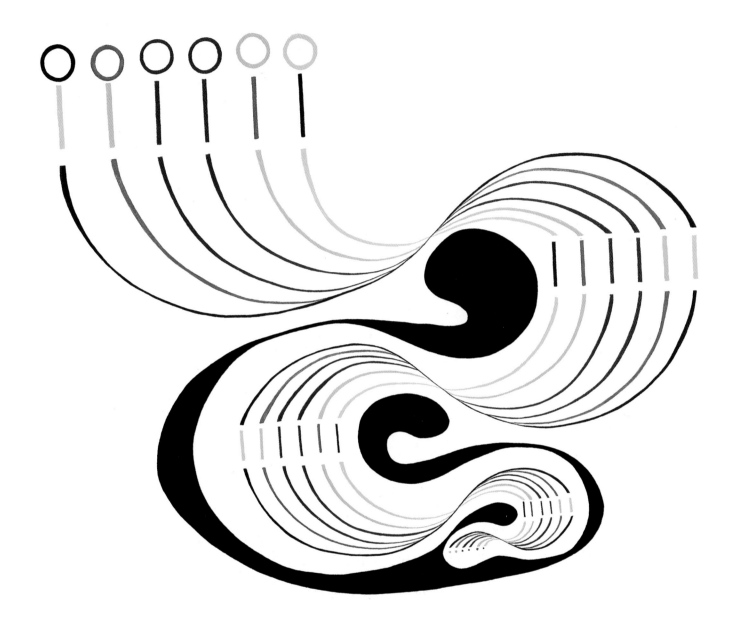

Author's Acknowledgements

Thanks to

Anna's family, the Tátrais;

Meredith McNabe and the Minnesota Medical Association
for the stimulation and opportunity to publish my thoughts and
art work in *Minnesota Medicine;*

Mary Ellen Gee for constant support and editorial assistance;

Candy Ames for encouraging this endeavor;

Erwin A. Kelen for establishment of
the *Yellow Star* Foundation.